LONDON CRAFT BEER
Over 50 Breweries and Brewery Taprooms to Visit in London

With grateful thanks to Trevor Parkes, Michael Kendall, Michael Potter and Lee Barnes.

Cover photo: Howling Hops, Hackney Wick

If you would like to suggest a bar for inclusion or provide updated information regarding an entry please email feedback@nssales.co.uk

In the last few years London has become a thriving brewing capital, with dozens of interesting craft breweries and taprooms opening up. It now seems amazing that according to the yearly Good Beer Guide there were only 5 independent breweries located in London in 1999, and as recently as 2008 the publication only listed 11. Now London is estimated to have over 100. It really is a fantastic time to be a beer drinker.

The aim of this informal guide is to provide a list of the breweries that either offer a brewery tour and/or have a taproom, so you can see where the beer you are drinking is actually brewed and taste the liquid gold literally direct from the source.

Obviously with such a fast moving brewing scene it is difficult to keep up with the comings and goings of breweries that seem to change daily. We have done our best to compile a list that, to the best of our knowledge, is correct at time of going to press. We will aim to update the book annually to make any amendments, but in the meantime we recommend you check the brewery website before you visit, just in case there have been any changes.

You'll find the breweries listed in alphabetical order, but to aid your interest in visiting them we have provided a public transport index at the back listing the nearest Tube, DLR, London Overground or National Rail Train Stations to each brewery. After each brewery we've also provided a What's Nearby section noting any other craft breweries or interesting pubs located close by, just in case you want to make a day of it.

We hope you find the guide helpful and informative. If you would like to suggest a brewery for inclusion or provide updated information regarding an entry please feel free to email us at feedback@nssales.co.uk

ALPHABETA BREWERY, Pitt Cue, 1 The Avenue, Devonshire Sq, EC2M 4YP. Approximately 10 minutes walk to Aldgate Tube or Liverpool Street Tube and National Rail Train Station. The brewery is located inside the Pitt Cue bar and restaurant which is open 12noon to 11pm Monday to Friday and 6pm to 11pm Saturday. www.alphabetabrewery.com

Pitt Cue started out in 2011 as a food truck on the Southbank of the River Thames specialising in grilled meats. It hasn't done badly to now have this impressive restaurant in the heart of the city's business district. Housed inside the bar/restaurant is their own in-house microbrewery that produces a regularly changing range of small-batch beers. These have included a Pale Ale, Oak aged ale, Rye beer and a smoked porter. You don't need to eat there, you can just go in for a drink at the bar, but the food is rather good.

NEARBY: A 15 minute walk to the other side of Liverpool street you'll find The Long Arm Brew Pub at 20-26 Worship Street, Shoreditch, EC2A 2DX. This impressive brewpub set-up serves 6 beers pumped directly from giant tanks straight to the glass. www.longarmpub.com.

The Crosse Keys, 9 Gracechurch St, EC3V 0DR is around a 10 minute walk from Pitt Cue. This impressive branch of the Wetherspoons pub chain is housed in a former bank, with many of the grand features from the building still maintained. You'll find around 12 real ales available on draft as well as a good selection of keg and bottled beers.

ANSPACH & HOBDAY, 118 Druid Street, Bermondsey, SE1 2HH. Approximately 10 minutes walk to Bermondsey Tube or 20 minutes walk to London Bridge Tube and National Rail Train Station. Taproom open Friday 5pm to 9pm, Saturday 10.30am to 6.30pm and Sunday 12.30pm to 5pm. www.anspachandhobday.com

You'll find the Anspatch & Hobday microbrewery located on the Bermondsey Beer Mile, which refers to the large amount of breweries situated close together in railway arches and industrial units in that area of London. Why do a pub crawl when you can visit a series of excellent taprooms serving lovely fresh beer! Visiting the Anspatch & Hobday brewery you'll find around 8 different beers on draft as well as a selection of bottles. The core range comprises of the usual IPA, Pale Ale and Porter styles, but A&H are very proactive in trying new recipes, so you'll frequently discover interesting experimental brews that they have been working on. Brewery tours and other special events are held occasionally, check their website for details.

NEARBY: The fantastic Bermondsey Bottle Shop is located just a few arches away at 128 Druid St, SE1 2HH. Open Friday to Sunday this beer bar and shop normally offers 12 beers on tap and 400 in bottles. See their website for full details: www.bottleshop.co.uk
Additionally there are four other brewery taps within 5 minutes walk; Hiver Beers, 56 Stanworth St, Bermondsey SE1 3NY; Southwalk Brewing Company, 46 Druid St, SE1 2EZ; Brew By Numbers, 79 Enid St, SE16 3RA; UBREW, Old Jamaica Business Estate, 29 Old Jamaica Rd, SE16 4AW. If you fancy a craft cider or ginger beer you'll also find Hawkes Cidery at 96 Druid St, SE1 2HQ.

THE BARNET BREWERY, The Black Horse, 92 Wood Street, High Barnet, EN5 4BW. Approximately 15 minute walk from High Barnet Tube. Brewery tours are not currently offered. www.blackhorsebarnet.co.uk
The Barnet Brewery are based out the back of The Black Horse Pub, you can see the set-up if you go into the beer garden at the rear. The pub acts as the taproom for the brewery with 8 real ales on draft, of which up to 4 will be their own beers. The styles are normally likeable session drinks such as their Barnet Best and Barnet Blonde. You'll also find a good food menu available. As an aside, the brewing equipment being used was originally from the Federation Brewery in Newcastle Upon Tyne. They used to brew Newcastle Brown Ale, before it was closed down by new owners Heineken in 2010 and production moved to their John Smith's Brewery in Tadcaster, North Yorkshire.

NEARBY: There are a number of old historic coaching inns in Barnet with Ye Olde Mitre Inne at 58 High Street, High Barnet, EN5 5SJ, being the oldest. Records show there has been a pub on the site since 1553. You'll find the pub a 10 minute walk away from The Black Horse. A choice of 8 real ales are available on draft and food is served. www.facebook.com/yeoldemitreinn

The Butchers Arms is also a 10 minute walk from the brewery at 148 High Street, High Barnet, EN5 5XP. This popular former Wetherspoon's pub normally has 5 real ales available.

BELLEVIILE BREWING COMPANY, 36 Jaggard Way, Balham, SW12 8SG. Approximately 2 minutes walk from Wandsworth Common National Rail Train Station. Alternatively a 15 minute walk to Balham Tube. Brewery shop open for take-away bottles/cans on Monday to Friday 9am to 4pm. Taproom open Friday 5pm to 8pm and Saturday 12noon to 8pm. Opening times may vary, check their website for latest details. Brewery tours are not currently offered. www.bellevillebrewing.co.uk

The Belleville Brewing Company was founded in 2013 by a group of fathers whose children all attended the Belleville primary school in south west London. Being fans of American style craft beers their inspiration is based on the adage "Beers from over there, brewed over here", so the range includes hoppy IPA's, Rye, Amber and Pale Ales. They also brew a number of seasonal beers to total 15 styles in total throughout the year, including a tasty wheat beer, black lager and a porter. You'll normally find around 8 beers available on draft in their taproom plus a selection of cans and bottles.

NEARBY: The impressive off-licence/bar We Brought Beer, 28 Hildreth St, Balham, SW12 9RQ is around a 20 minute walk away. This specialist beer shop is part of a small chain, and stocks around 400 different beers in bottles and cans along with 4 ever-changing beers on draft. All drinks can be drunk in store or taken away. They regularly hold special events at their stores, such as tasting sessions and meet the brewer, see their website for details. www.webroughtbeer.co.uk

If you enjoy American craft beers you'll find the Goose Island Vintage Ale House also in Balham at 3 Ramsden Road, SW12 8QY. Owned by the Chicago based Goose Island Brewery (who are additionally now owned by a multinational conglomerate) this bar brings a little bit of Americana to the back streets of South London. If you're looking for something a bit different they offer an exclusive range of Goose Island beers and a good food menu. www.gooseisland.com/vintagealehouse-balham

BEVERTOWN BREWERY, Units 17 & 18 Lockwood Industrial Park, Mill Mead Road, Tottenham Hale, N17 9QP. Approximately 10 minutes walk to Tottenham Hale Tube or London Overground stations. Taproom open Saturday 2pm to 8pm. Brewery tours are not currently held, although there are regular events and beer launches at the brewery and the brewing equipment is on display, see website for details. www.beavertownbrewery.co.uk Bevertown's brightly decorated cans and catchily named drinks have become a regular fixture on the craft beer scene. Names such as Gamma Ray, Neck Oil and Smog Rocket stick in the consciousness, along with artwork that draws inspiration from graphic novels, old Star Wars comics and cult b-movies, but it also helps that they also brew rather good beer. The brewery/taproom is located in a pretty unremarkable industrial park in north London, but it's worth the trip as you'll find around 10 of their beers on draft along with a range of bottles and cans. There is also a selection of street food on offer. Due to their popularity, if they are holding a beer launch or special event on a particular Saturday the taproom will be ticketed entry only, so be sure to check their website before you travel.

NEARBY: The Beehive, Stoneleigh Road, N17 9BQ. This large Tudor-style pub is often heralded for its historic interior that has hardly altered since 1927. It's about a 20 minute walk from the Bevertown Brewery and if you're thirsty after the stroll you'll find around 7 real ales on draft

as well as a good selection of craft beers. Good home-cooked food is also available. www.beehiven17.com
Another old traditional pub nearby is the Ferry Boat Inn, a 10 minute walk from the brewery at Ferry Lane, N17 9NG. Located on the banks of the Low Maynard reservoir this large pub offers 5 real ales on draft, a nice beer garden and a good food menu. www.theferryboatlondon.co.uk

BEXLEY BREWERY, 18 Manford Industrial Estate, Manor Road, Erith, DA8 2AJ. Approximately 20 minutes walk from Slade Green National Rail Train Station. Alternatively a 25 minute walk from Erith National Rail Train Station. The 99 bus route also runs from Woolwich Arsenal DLR station and stops at the brewery. This bus route also passes Erith and Slade Green if you don't fancy the walk from either train station. Taproom and shop are normally open every Friday (12noon to 5pm) and Saturday (12noon to 3pm) although these times are subject to change. Check their website for latest details. Brewery tours are held one Saturday every other month, see website for details. www.bexleybrewery.co.uk
The Bexley Brewery was formed in 2014 by the home-brewing husband and wife team of Cliff and Jane Murphy. It finally brought a brewery back to the Bexley area of London for the first time since 1956 when Reffells Bexley was taken over by Courage & Co Ltd who subsequently closed them down. The new brewery produce 6 core beers including a Golden Ale, Ruby Ale and Pale Ale, as well as 4 seasonal beers and the occasional one-off. You'll usually find 5 available straight from the cask when the taproom is open along with the full range available in bottles.

NEARBY: Sadly near the brewery there is rather a shortage of decent pubs however if you head to Slade Green station and travel the short distance (or catch the 428 bus) to Crayford you'll find the Penny Farthing at 3 Waterside, Crayford, DA1 4JJ. This delightful micro pub is located in a former bicycle shop, hence the name, and typically serves 6 real ales directly from the barrel, along with 2 real ciders. Be warned though, if your mobile phone rings you'll be fined £1 towards a local charity. www.pennyfarthingcrayford.co.uk

BIG SMOKE BREW CO. 87 Maple Rd, Surbiton KT6 4AW. Approximately 10 minutes walk from Surbiton National Rail Train Station. The brewery is located at the rear of The Antelope pub which is open Monday to Thursday 12noon to 11pm, Friday and Saturday 12noon to 11.30pm and Sunday 12noon to 10.30pm. Brewery tours are not currently held. www.bigsmokebrew.co.uk and www.theantelope.co.uk

Started in 2014, the Big Smoke Brew Co. are located in formed stables at the rear of The Antelope pub in Surbiton, which acts as the taproom for the brewery. Big Smoke produce 7 core beers including Electric Eye Pale Ale, Bonfire Bitter and Underworld Milk Stout. The beers are normally brewed without finings (commonly a fish based product used to clear the liquid) which means they can be naturally hazy and generally vegan friendly. You'll normally find 10 real ales, 5 real ciders & 8 keg beers available at the bar, which will include drinks from the Big Smoke range with a selection of guest beers. A variety of bottled and canned beers are also available. Food is served, which is predominately tasty steaks and burgers. The brewery also own another local pub, The Albion, 45 Fairfield Road, Kingston, KT1 2PY, so you'll find a selection of their beers served there as well.

NEARBY: The Lamb, 73 Brighton Road, KT6 5NF is about a 5 minute walk from The Antelope. This friendly backstreet pub offers a good selection of real ale. They are also rather passionate about their cheeses with a 3 cheese ploughman's lunch normally available.

In the other direction you'll find the Waggon & Horses, 1 Surbiton Hill Road, KT6 4TW is about a 10 minute walk from The Albion. This historic old pub offers a decent selection of ales normally from across the Wells & Youngs range. A good range of food is also served.

BOHEM BREWERY, 120a Myddleton Rd, London N22 8NQ. Approximately 5 minutes walk to Bowes Park

National Rail or 10 minutes walk to Bounds Green Tube. Taproom open daily Monday to Thursday 5pm to 11pm and Friday to Sunday 4pm to 11pm. Brewery tours are not currently offered, but the taproom does hold tasting events throughout the year, see their website for details. www.bohembrewery.com.

This new brewery was opened in 2015 by friends Zdenek Kudr and Petr Skocek. Their mission is to only brew Bohemian lagers, that is to mean Czech craft beers brewed by a Czech brewer using Czech ingredients. The results are very impressive with the regular lines including a tasty Pale, Amber, Pilsner, Black lager and a Honey lager. The concept has proved so popular that they have already outgrown their original premises with the beer now brewed at a site in Edmonton about 3 miles away from the Taproom.

NEARBY: Just over a 10 minute walk from the taproom and highly recommended for a visit is The Prince, 1 Finsbury Road, Wood Green, N22 8PA. This local pub has been totally rejuvenated since a change of ownership in 2016. It now serves 6 rotating real ales and 7 keg beers on draft. The choice normally includes an option from their in-house microbrewery (named the **HOUSE BREWERY**) such as their 3% Table Beer or 6% APA. Meals are available Thursday to Sunday with snacks served Monday to Wednesday. www.theprincen22.co.uk and www.housebrewery.co.uk.

The Ranelagh, 82 Bounds Green Road, N11 2EU is also around a 10 minute walk from the taproom. This large, historic pub offers a good range of craft beers with food served all day. www.theranelaghn11.co.uk

BREW BY NUMBERS, 79 Enid St, Bermondsey SE16 3RA. Approximately 10 minutes walk to Bermondsey Tube or 20 minutes walk to London Bridge Tube and National Rail Train Stations. Taproom open Friday 6pm to 10pm and Saturday 11am to 8pm. Closed Sunday to Thursday. Brewery tours are not currently offered, but BBNo do hold regular special events at the brewery throughout the year, see their website for details. www.brewbynumbers.com

BBNo are an experimental brewery that have created a large number of beers since they started out in 2012. You'll notice all their beers are given a unique number e.g. 04:02, the first digits refer to the beer style and the second to the recipe number they are attempting. They currently brew over 25 styles of beer from Amber Ale to Session IPA to Witbier and they have experimented with a good number of recipes across these, so you'll always find something new to try. The taproom typically has 12 beers on draft along with a selection of bottles. In common with several other entries in this book BBNo's is located on the Bermondsey Beer Mile, a term that refers to the large amount of taprooms located close together in that area of London.

NEARBY: The Bermondsey Bottle Shop is located a few minutes' walk away at 128 Druid St, London SE1 2HH. Open Friday to Sunday this beer bar and shop normally has 12 different beers on tap and 400 in bottles. See their website for full details: www.bottleshop.co.uk
Additionally there are several other brewery taps within 10-15 minute walk; UBREW, Old Jamaica Business Estate, 29 Old Jamaica Rd, SE16 4AW; Anspach & Hobday, 118 Druid Street, Bermondsey, SE1 2HH; Partizan Brewing, 8 Almond Rd, Bermondsey SE16 3LR.
The Kernel Brewery, Arch 11 Dockley Road Industrial Estate, SE16 3SF is also about a 5 minute walk. Sadly they do not have a taproom or tour, but they are open Saturday 9am to 2pm selling bottles to take-away. www.thekernelbrewery.com

BREWHOUSE AND KITCHEN HIGHBURY, 2a Corsica Street, N5 1JJ. Approximately 5 minutes walk from Highbury & Islington Tube, London Overground and National Rail Train Station. Bar is open Monday to Thursday 11am to 11pm, Friday and Saturday 11am to midnight and Sunday 12noon to 11pm. Brewery Experience Days and Tutored Beer Tasting Sessions can be booked online through their website. www.brewhouseandkitchen.com
Brewhouse and Kitchen are a chain of pubs that brew their own beers onsite. The Brewer for each particular branch is

given freedom to brew their own recipes and although some successful beers are shared throughout the chain, you'll always find exclusive brews in each pub. In addition to their house beers you'll also find an impressive collection of craft and international beers on draft and in bottles. Beer masterclasses are held several times a week in which you have a tutored tasting of 8 different styles of beer. If you prefer the full-on brewery experience though you can book to spend a whole day with the Brewer and create your own beer. Details for these can be found on their website. Food is available. It's around a 25minute walk or short bus ride to the other London Brewhouse and Kitchen bar at Angel Islington.

NEARBY: The Hammerton Brewery is around a 15minute walk away at Unit 8 & 9 Roman Way Industrial Estate, 149 Roman Way, N7 8XH. This popular micro-brewery holds a taproom open day once a month, but more conveniently has opened its first pub around a 10 minute walk from the Brewhouse and Kitchen. The House of Hammerton, 97-99 Holloway Road, N7 8LT serves over 20 beers on draft including its own range and choice guests, and you'll also find over 50 bottles/cans available. www.hammertonbrewery.co.uk

A bit further up Holloway Road is The Lamb pub, 54 Holloway Road N7 8JL. This historic old boozer dates from the 1870's and you'll always find a good selection of craft beers and real ale available. Food is provided by a local pizzeria. www.thelambn7.co.uk

In the other direction The Taproom, 163 Upper St, N1 1US is about a 15 minute walk from the Brewhouse. This specialist beer bar is well worth checking out, with up to 8 real ales, 7 keg beers and a large selection of bottles and cans. Food is also available. www.thetaprooms.co.uk

BREWHOUSE AND KITCHEN ISLINGTON, Torrens Street, London, EC1V 1NQ. Approximately 5 minutes walk from Angel Tube. Bar is open Monday to Thursday 11am to 11pm, Friday 11am to midnight, Saturday 10am to midnight and Sunday 10am to 10.30pm. Brewery Experience Days and Tutored Beer Tasting Sessions can be booked through their website. www.brewhouseandkitchen.com

Brewhouse and Kitchen are a chain of pubs that brew their own beers in a onsite microbrewery. The Brewer for each particular branch is given freedom to brew their own recipes and although some successful beers are shared amongst the chain, you'll always find exclusive brews in each pub. In addition to their house beers you'll find an impressive collection of craft and international beers on draft and in bottles. Beer masterclasses are held several times a week in which you have a tutored tasting of 8 different styles of beer. If you prefer the full-on brewery experience though you can book to spend a whole day with the Brewer and create your own beer. Details for these can be found on their website. Food is available. It's around a 25minute walk or short bus ride to the other London Brewhouse and Kitchen bar at Highbury.

NEARBY: The Old Red Lion, 418 St John Street, EC1V 4NJ is just across the street and around the corner from the Brewhouse and Kitchen. This old fashioned pub can trace its roots back to 1415 and is one of the oldest surviving drinking establishments in London. You'll always find some interesting ales on draft and food is available. www.oldredliontheatre.co.uk

The Craft Beer Co., 55 White Lion Street, N1 9PP is a pub about 10 minutes walk away that stocks an amazing selection of beers. You'll normally find around 35 different choices on draft with another in 200 bottles or cans. Food is also available. www.thecraftbeerco.com

The Taproom, 163 Upper St, N1 1US is a 15 minute walk from the brewery. This specialist beer bar is also well worth checking out, with up to 8 real ales, 7 keg beers and a large selection of bottles and cans. Food is available. www.thetaprooms.co.uk

BRICK BREWERY, Arch 209, Blenheim Grove, Peckham, SE15 4QL. Located in a railway arch approximately 2 minutes walk from Peckham Rye London Overground and National Rail Train Station. Taproom open Wednesday 5pm to 9pm, Thursday & Friday 5pm to 10pm and Saturday 12noon to 10pm. Brewery tours are possible,

drop them an email to enquire if you are interested.
www.brickbrewery.co.uk
Since starting out in a Peckham shed in 2013 the Brick
Brewery have come a long way, creating a decent
brewery, taproom and impressive range of beers. In the
taproom you'll find around 9 different beers on draft and a
selection of bottles and cans. The Red Brick Rye and
Blenheim Black are particular favourites from the core
range and their experimental brews have included
American IPA's and a Rhubarb Sour beer. Food is
provided by Slow Richie's kitchen serving burgers and
BBQ. Take note that most of the seating area is outside so
the weather can play a factor when visiting.

NEARBY: If you fancy something a bit different the
Gosnells Mead Brewery is around a 5 minute walk away at
Unit 2, Print Village, Chadwick Rd, Peckham SE15 4PU.
This brewery, or should we say meadery, produces a
range of fermented honey drinks. Their taproom is open on
Saturdays from 12noon to 8pm so you can give them a try.
www.gosnells.co.uk
For more beer, situated a 5 minute walk away from the
Brick Brewery you'll find John the Unicorn at 157-159 Rye
Lane, SE15 4TL. This unusually named pub is owned by
the Antic Group who in turn own the Croydon based
Volden Brewery, so you'll find their range on draft along
with a selection of guest and craft beers. Food is also
served. www.johntheunicorn.com. Sadly Volden don't have
a taproom or brewery tour, but their beers are definitely
worth a try if you come across one of their predominately
South London Antic pubs.
Four Quarters, 187 Rye Lane, SE15 4TP is also just a 5 or
10 minute walk away from the Brick Brewery. This oddity
can best be described as a retro games arcade with a craft
beer bar. So if you fancy a game of Sonic or Space
Invaders while enjoying a pint, then this really is the ideal
place to go. There are normally 5 beers on draft and 40
available in bottles or cans. Food is available.
www.fourquartersbar.co.uk

BRIXTON BREWERY, Arch 547, Brixton Station Road, SW9 8PF. Approximately 5 minutes walk to Brixton Tube and National Rail Train Stations. Alternatively the brewery is a 10 minute walk to Loughborough Junction National Rail Train Station. Taproom and Shop open Friday 6pm to 10pm and Saturday 12noon to 6pm. Brewery tours and beer tasting sessions are often suspended during July and August due to brewing schedules, but are held regularly the rest of the year. See website for booking details. www.brixtonbrewery.com

Like many others breweries the Brixton Brewery are located in an arch behind a station. One can only imagine that the railway arches of London would have a glut of rental vacancies if it wasn't for the thriving microbrewery scene. Just a short walk from Brixton's vibrant market the Brixton Brewery started in 2013 and have now developed a core range concentrating on full-flavour styles such as their Atlantic APA and Electric IPA. They have also produced a number of collaborations and small batch one-off beers, many of which you'll probably only get a chance to try on draft if you visit their taproom. Beers are also available in bottles to take away.

NEARBY: Another brewery, Clarkshaws, is located about a 10 minute walk away at 497 Ridgway Rd, Brixton, SW9 7EX. Their taproom is open Friday and Saturday where you'll find their Vegetarian Society approved, with all UK sourced ingredients, range of beers available. www.clarkshaws.co.uk

A few minutes' walk back towards the station from the Brixton Brewery and you'll discover The Craft Beer Co pub at 11-13 Brixton Station Rd, SW9 8PA. This small chain of pubs always offer a fantastic range of beers and the Brixton branch is one of the best. You'll find around 30 beers on draft and over 200 in bottles and cans.

You really are spoilt for choice in this area as The Crown and Anchor, 246 Brixton Rd, SW9 6AQ is just a 15 minute walk away. Again this is part of a small chain of pubs that are concentrating on offering an impressive range of beers, with around 25 taps and a selection of bottles available. A good food menu is also served.

BROCKLEY BREWERY COMPANY, 31 Harcourt Rd, Brockley, SE4 2AJ. Approximately 5 minutes walk from Brockley London Overground and National Rail Train Station. Taproom and bottle shop open Friday 5.30pm to 9pm and Saturday 12noon to 9pm. Brewery tours are not currently held but brewing equipment is on display at the taproom. www.brockleybrewery.co.uk

The Brockley Brewery Company micro brewery is based in a rather nondescript industrial unit in the back streets of south east London. They currently produce 5 regular beers; Golden Ale, Pale Ale, Porter, Red Ale and IPA, along with seasonal brews such as a Summer Ale and one-off beers like the recent Rum-Plum Porter. You'll find a friendly welcome at their brewery taproom along with their full range of beers on draft as well as available to take-away in bottles. Various Street Food vendors are often on-site cooking up fresh food, check their website or Facebook/Twitter page for the latest information.

NEARBY: The Brockley Barge at 184 Brockley Road, SE4 2RR is a large unpretentious Wetherspoon's pub around a 5 minute walk away. They offer 10 real ales on draft and the usual food menu. www.jdwetherspoon.com

The London Beer Dispensary is a 15 minute walk from the brewery at 389 Brockley Rd, SE4 2PH. Owned by the Penge based Southey Brewing Company this bar without a bar (yes, there really is no conventional bar counter), serves up an impressive selection of beers straight from the barrel/cask. There is also a good range of bottles and canned beers available along with tasty burgers. www.facebook.com/LDNDispensary

BULLFINCH BREWERY, Arch 886, Rosendale Rd, Herne Hill, SE24 9EH. Approximately 10 minutes walk to Herne Hill National Rail Train Station or a 20 minute walk to North Dulwich, Tulse Hill or West Dulwich National Rail Train Stations. Alternatively a 30 minute walk from Brixton Tube station. Taproom open Wednesday to Friday 4pm to 10pm, Saturday & Sunday 12noon to 10pm. Closed Monday and Tuesday. Brewery tours are not currently held. www.thebullfinchbrewery.co.uk

Formed in 2014 this modern microbrewery give a nod to the traditional by brewing on a historic 5 barrel kit originally built by Charles Wells. In the taproom you'll find 12 beers on tap which include core Bullfinch lines such as Rascal Session IPA, Luna Light Pale Ale and Wolf American Pale Ale. They also stock a range of limited edition experimental brews, a couple of guest beers from other local brewers and a range of bottles.

NEARBY: A 5 minute walk will lead you to the Canopy Brewing Company similarly located under the railway tracks at Arch 1127, Bath Factory Estate, 41 Norwood Rd, SE24 9AJ. If you're still thirsty after Bullfinch you'll find another 12 beers on draft in the Canopy taproom. www.canopybeer.com

After all that drinking if you're feeling hungry The Florence gastropub is a 10 minute walk at 131-133 Dulwich Rd, SE24 0NG. This popular pub usually has 4 different real ales on draft. It also features its own very small microbrewery onsite, so you may find one of their own beers available if they have been brewing. www.florenceherne hill.com

BY THE HORNS BREWING COMPANY, 25 Summerstown, Tooting/Wimbledon SW17 0BQ. Approximately 20 minutes walk to Tooting Broadway Tube or a 25 minute walk to Wimbledon Park Tube. Alternatively the brewery is a 15 minute walk to Haydons Road National Rail Train Station. Taproom is open Tuesday to Thursday 4pm to 11pm, Friday 4pm to 11.30pm, Saturday 12noon to 11.30pm and Sunday 2pm to 11pm. Closed Monday. Brewery tours are not currently held regularly, however that can be pre-arranged for groups if you drop them an email. www.bythehorns.co.uk

Based in bright blue industrial units in South West London, By the Horns was formed in 2011, making it one of the older brewers in the new wave of London microbreweries. Their core beers include Wolfie Smith Amber IPA, Mayor of Garratt Best Bitter and Stiff Upper Lip Pale Ale. In addition they produce a number of seasonal and special brews. In the taproom you'll normally find 3 of their real ales on pump, up to 9 keg beers and a number of bottles. Food isn't generally available apart from bar snacks. Major sporting events are often shown on large projector screens and it can get busy during when these are showing, so it is advisable to book yourself some seats through their website.

NEARBY: The Leather Bottle, 538 Garratt Lane, Summerstown, SW17 0NY. A 15 minute walk from the brewery leads you to this historic pub dating from the 17th Century. Now part of the Young's chain the beer is limited to their stable, but if the weather is hot there is a very nice beer garden to enjoy and a rather good food menu. www.leatherbottlepub.co.uk
If you're heading towards Tooting Broadway you'll find the fantastic off-licence/bar We Brought Beer at 21-23 Tooting High St, SW17 0SN, around a 20 minute walk from the brewery. This specialist beer shop is part of a small chain and stocks around 200 different beers in bottles and cans along with 3 ever-changing beers on draft. All can be drunk in store or taken away. www.webroughtbeer.co.uk

CAMDEN TOWN BREWERY, 55-59 Wilkin Street Mews, Camden, NW5 3NN. A couple of minutes walk from Kentish Town West London Overground station. Alternatively it's approximately 15 minutes walk from Chalk Farm Tube or a 20 minute walk from Camden Town Tube stations. The brewery Taproom is open Sunday to Thursday 1pm to 9pm, Friday 1pm to 11pm and Saturday 12noon to 9pm. Brewery tours are held every week, normally on Thursday and Saturday, see website for details and to book. www.camdentownbrewery.com
Since starting out in 2010 The Camden Town Brewery soon become a major player on the emerging craft beer scene. The initial plan was to produce a decent German style lager rather than the usual gold pish served up as lager in many UK pubs. The result was their Camden Hells and the success of this showed they had definitely found a gap in the market. The core range now includes a Pale Ale, Wheat beer, Pils and Stout, alongside a number of seasonal and one-off creations. You'll find the full range

available on draft at the railway arched taproom bar at their Camden based brewery. In similarity with Meantime the breweries "craft" credentials took a bit of a knock when they were bought by international drinks conglomerate Anheuser-Busch InBev in 2015. Presumably as a result of this take-over a major investment was made to build a very large new brewery in Enfield, 12 miles away from the original site, which opened in 2017. The Camden brewery is still kept in operation, but mainly for one-off beers and collaborations. Brewery tours are available at both sites and can be booked through their website. The Enfield brewery address is Camden Town Brewery, Morson Road, Enfield EN3 4TJ, which is about a 10 minute walk from Ponders End National Rail Train Station or a 25 minute walk to Southbury London Overground Station.

NEARBY: Less than 5 minutes walk from the Camden brewery you'll find The Grafton at 20 Prince of Wales Road, Kentish Town, NW5 3LG. This award winning pub always has a good range of beers on draft as well as a good selection of bottles and cans. Food is available. www.thegraftonnw5.co.uk
A 20 minute walk will take you to BrewDog Camden at 113 Bayham St, NW1 0AG. This outlet for the popular Scottish brewery serves around 17 beers on draft, many from the BrewDog range, but also unusual guest beers. There is also around 100 beers available in bottles and cans. You won't find anything from the local Camden Town brewery though, as BrewDog announced they would stop stocking their beers once they were taken over by AB InBev. www.brewdog.com
If you are visiting the Enfield brewery the Picture Palace, Howard Hall, Lincoln Road, Ponders End, EN3 4AQ is about a 20 minute walk away. This pub, inside a converted 1913 cinema, normally has a good selection of beers and food is served all day. www.facebook.com/picturepalace01

CANOPY BEER COMPANY, Arch 1127, Bath Factory Estate, 41 Norwood Rd, Herne Hill, SE24 9AJ. Approximately 5 minutes walk to Herne Hill National Rail Train Station or 15 minutes walk to North Dulwich National

Rail Train Station. Alternatively a 25 minute walk from Brixton Tube station. Taproom open Wednesday to Friday 5pm to 11pm, Saturday 12noon to 11pm and Sunday 12noon to 10pm. Closed Monday and Tuesday. Brewery tours are not currently held, although all the brewing equipment is on display in the taproom. www.canopybeer.com

Canopy are a small microbrewery formed in 2014 and located in a secluded railway arch near Herne Hill. The core beer range consist of Brockwell IPA, Sunray Pale Ale, Tall Trees Session IPA and Milkwood Amber, but in addition they product a large number of small batch experimental brews. If you can find it, the lively taproom is well worth a visit, there is normally 10 beers on keg and two real ale hand pumps as well as a number of bottles. Occasional brewery tours are held, check out the news section on their website for details.

NEARBY: If you're feeling hungry The Florence gastro-pub is a 5 minute walk at 131-133 Dulwich Rd, SE24 0NG. They normally have 4 different real ales on draft and also feature their own very small microbrewery on site, so you may find one of their own beers available if they have been brewing. www.florenceherneHill.com

A 5 minute walk in the other direction from the Canopy Brewery will lead you to the Bullfinch Brewery, Arch 886, Rosendale Rd, SE24 9EH. Located in another railway arch down the road, you'll find up to 12 different beers available on draft in their taproom.

CLARKSHAWS BREWERY, 497 Ridgway Rd, Brixton, SW9 7EX. Approximately 15 minutes walk from Brixton Tube and National Rail Train Station. Alternatively a 5 minute walk from Loughborough Junction National Rail Train Station. Taproom open every Friday and Saturday 12noon to 8pm. Regular brewery tours are not currently held, but the brewery does have live brew open days and also the opportunity to be a brewer for a day, see their website for details. www.clarkshaws.co.uk

Located in a railway arch not far from the nearby Brixton Brewery, Clarkshaws are an independent microbrewery opened in 2013, initially in Dulwich, then expanding to their current site in 2015. They were proudly London's first micro to produce all Vegetarian Society accredited products and they also only brew using UK ingredients, so you won't find their beers crammed with American hops, as is often the fashion. Their core brews include Gorgon's Alive Golden Ale, Strange Brew No.1 English Pale Ale, Phoenix Rising Ruby Ale and Hellbound IPA (which is crammed with UK hops). The brewery is often open additional days rather than just Friday and Saturday, check the events page on their website for details.

NEARBY: As mentioned the Brixton Brewery is about a 5-10 minute walk away at Arch 547, Brixton Station Road, SW9 8PF. Their taproom is open on Friday and Saturday, where you'll find their range of full-on flavour, hoppy beers available to try. www.brixtonbrewery.com
A few minutes' walk past The Brixton Brewery you'll find The Craft Beer Co pub at 11-13 Brixton Station Rd, SW9 8PA. This small chain of pubs always offer a fantastic range of beers and the Brixton branch is one of the best. You'll find around 30 beers on draft and over 200 in bottles and cans to choose from.
Craft beer specialist Ghost Whale is a 15 minute walk from Clarkshaws at 70 Atlantic Rd, Brixton, SW9 8PX. This former hairdressers has been transformed into a fabulous bar/off-license with 4 beers on draft and around 300 available in bottles and cans.

CRATE BREWERY, Unit 7, Queens Yard, Hackney Wick, E9 5EN. Approximately 5 minutes walk to Hackney Wick London Overground. Alternatively a 20 minute walk from Stratford Tube, DLR, London Overground and National Rail Train Station or Stratford International DLR and National Rail Train Station or Homerton London Overground station. Taproom open Sunday to Thursday 12noon to 11pm and Friday & Saturday 12noon to midnight. Tours are regularly held on Thursdays and Saturdays, see website for details. www.cratebrewery.com
You'll find the Crate Brewery located by the canal that runs alongside the Queen Elizabeth Olympic Park. This

provides a lovely setting to visit during the summer where you can sit outside, enjoy a pint and watch the narrow boats sail by. Brewery tours are held, but need to be booked in advance. If you just want to try the beer you can turn up to their lively taproom and you'll find Crate's regular IPA, Pale and Lager on draft along with some limited editions and guest beers. The bar also specialises in interesting stone-baked pizzas which are well worth trying.

NEARBY: Howling Hops Brewery is located on the same industrial park at Unit 9, Queens Yard, White Post Lane, E9 5EN. It would be rude not to also visit them while you are in the area.
The Hackney based brewery Five Points owns the Mason and Company bar a 15 minute walk away on the opposite side of the canal at 25 East Bay Lane, Here East, Queen Elizabeth Olympic Park, E20 3BS. This impressive craft beer bar stocks around 20 types on draft along with a large range of cans and bottles.

DRAGONFLY BREWERY, The George & Dragon, 183 High St, Acton, W3 9DJ. Approximately 15 minutes walk to Acton Town Tube. Alternatively a 10 minute walk to Acton Central on the London Overground. The Dragonfly Brewery is located inside The George & Dragon pub which is open Monday to Wednesday 4pm to 11pm, Thursday 4pm to 11.45pm, Friday 4pm to 1am, Saturday 12noon to 1am and Sunday 12noon to 10.30pm. Brewery tours are not currently held. www.facebook.com/DragonflyActon
The Dragonfly Brewery is housed at the back of the George & Dragon pub, a 17th Century Inn that has had a major refurbishment to blend the old traditional features with the shiny new stainless steel of the 1200L brewing vessels housed at the rear. Beers are normally available on keg and cask with the core range including Achtung! Wheat Beer, Early Doors Oatmeal Pale Ale and Blighty Best, their traditional best bitter. In addition they produce a number of experimental and seasonal brews as well as stocking a good range of guest beers on draft and in bottles. Food is available and a live band performs jazz on Thursday nights.

Dragonfly Brewery, Acton

NEARBY: Further along the High Street you'll find The Red Lion & Pineapple at 281 High Street, W3 9BP. This large Wetherspoon's pub is fairly standard for the chain, but food is served all day and there's normally 8 real ales on draft so you can't grumble. www.jdwetherspoon.com

If you head in the other direction you'll come to Acton Park which contains a fantastic outdoor crazy golf course. Even better, the attached cafe is licensed to sell alcohol so you enjoy a pint of beer while playing your round of golf. www.puttinthepark.com/acton-park

ESSEX STREET BREWERY, Temple Brew House, 46 Essex St, Temple, WC2R 3JF. Approximately 5 minutes walk from Temple Tube station. Alternatively a 15 minute walk from Blackfriars Tube and National Rail Train Station. The micro-brewery is located inside the Temple Brew House Pub. The pub is open Monday to Wednesday 12noon to 11pm, Thursday 12noon to 11.30pm, Friday & Saturday 12noon to midnight and Sunday 12noon to 10.30pm. Brewery tours are flexibly held and can be booked through their website. www.templebrewhouse.com Located inside a former German theme pub, this basement bar now houses its own brewing equipment that you'll proudly see on display as you enter. The bar is owned by The City Pub Company who are building quite a reputation for running an impressive portfolio of pubs. These include similar Brew Houses containing microbreweries in Southampton, Norwich, Bath, Bristol and Cambridge. At this London branch you'll normally find 3 or 4 of their own Essex Street beers on draft along with 15 other craft beers and ciders on tap. There is also an impressive bottle/can list adding an additional 50 drinks to choose from. Food is also available. The brewery produce around 10 different beers in total, with core brews such as the TemPale and Dark Knight normally on tap along with a seasonal on rotation. Brewery tours with tastings are available to book through their website, with a VIP package also possible which includes a 3 course meal. Daly's Wine Bar located upstairs is more food & wine orientated, but is actually under the same ownership so you'll normally find a couple of the Essex Street beers on draft.

NEARBY: In this part of London there is no shortage of impressively historic pubs. Ye Olde Cheshire Cheese at 145 Fleet Street, EC4A 2BU (the entrance is down a side alleyway), is one of the most famous and located less than 10 minutes away. This Grade II listed building was built shortly after the Great Fire of London in 1666 and has been frequented over the years by the likes of Charles Dickens and PG Wodehouse . It's a bit of warren inside, but be sure to check out the rather unusual cellar bar. Beer wise the pub is owned by Samuel Smith's Yorkshire based Brewery so it only offers drinks for their own range. The stand out option of these, although only available in bottles and rather expensive, is the 8% Stingo, which has been aged for a year in oak casks. Well recommended if it is available.

Another interesting bar located nearby is the Black Friar, about a 15 minute walk at 174 Queen Victoria Street, EC4V 4EG. This Grade II pub was built in 1875 on the site of a Dominican friary. It was given a fabulous Art Nouveau makeover in 1905 and now contains fascinating sculptures, mosaics and reliefs throughout, depicting various friars. You'll find around 5 real ales on draft as well as a number of craft beers on keg and in cans/bottles. Food is available.

FIVE POINTS BREWING CO., 3 Institute Place, Hackney E8 1JE. Approximately 2 minutes walk from Hackney Downs National Rail Train Station or a 5 minute walk from Hackney Central London Overground Station. Brewery Tours and Tasting Sessions are held on the second Saturday each month at the brewery. Located about a mile away from the brewery is the Five Points Warehouse at 61 Mare Street, Hackney, E8 4RG. During the summer the warehouse opens the yard for Summer Tap Saturdays with Five Point beers, bands and street food. Details for tours and events can be found on their website. www.fivepointsbrewing.co.uk

Founded in 2013 the Five Points brewery produce 8 core beers; Five Points Pale, Hook Island Red, Railway Porter, Five Points IPA, Brick Field Brown, Five Points XPA, Five Points Pils and London Smoke, along with a number of seasonal and one-off brews. The majority of the beer is produced at their railway arched brewery in Hackney, but due to recent increases in demand some of the beer was outsourced to a family brewer in Belgium in 2016 while they try to find a way to expand the brewery. The monthly brewery tour is well worth booking but if the dates don't work out for you the brewery own the Mason and Company bar a couple of miles away at 25 East Bay Lane, Here East, Queen Elizabeth Olympic Park, E20 3BS. This impressive craft beer bar stocks around 20 beers on draft along with a large range of cans and bottles. Food is available from Capish an Italian-American street food kitchen.

NEARBY: A couple of minutes walk from the brewery is The Pembury Tavern, 90 Amhurst Rd, E8 1JH. This large pub is owned by the Cambridgeshire based Milton Brewery who produce an excellent range of real ales. You'll find twelve handpumps and nine keg taps serving the Milton collection along with guest beers from other microbreweries. www.individualpubs.co.uk/pembury

The Cock Tavern is around a 5 minute walk from the brewery at 315 Mare Street, E8 1EJ. This award winning pub has 24 taps that include a large range of cider as well as craft beer. The Maregade microbrewery is actually based in the pub basement. They don't offer tours but you'll normally find their latest brews on draft in the pub. www.thecocktavern.co.uk and www.maregade.com

40FT BREWERY, Bootyard, Abbott Street, Dalston, E8 3DP. Approximately 5 minutes walk from both Dalston Junction or Dalston Kingsland London Overground Stations. Brewery taproom open Friday and Saturday 5pm to 11pm. Brewery tours are not currently held. www.40ftbrewery.com

40FT Brewery who opened in 2015 are based in a disused car park in Dalston. If you're wondering about the name, let us explain; The brewery and taproom are built in repurposed 40 foot shipping containers. Yes it really is in a container. The Taproom is open every Friday and Saturday where you'll find their beers available on draft and in cans. Their core beers are Larger, a German style lager with a larger hoppier flavour, and Pale Ale, but they also produce a number of seasonal beers such as the recent Container Love IPA. There are often special events held at the taproom with bands and street food vendors, check their Facebook page for the latest news. www.facebook.com/40ftbrewery

NEARBY: The Railway Tavern Ale House is a 10 minute walk away at 2 St Jude Street, Dalston Kingsland, N16 8JT. This large beer-focused pub offers a good range of craft beers on draft and in bottles. Food is also available. www.facebook.com//RailwayTavernAleHouse

A ten minute walk in the other direction will take you to The Fox Craft Beer House at 372 Kingsland Rd, London E8 4DA. As the name suggests this friendly bar stocks 10 craft beers on draft with another 70 in bottles. Locally sourced food is also available. www.thefoxe8.com

FOURPURE BREWING, 22 Bermondsey Trading Estate, Rotherhithe New Rd, SE16 3LL. Approximately 15 minutes walk to Bermondsey Tube or 10 minutes walk to Surrey Quays London Overground station. Alternatively South Bermondsey National Rail Train Station is a couple of minutes away. Taproom open Friday 4pm to 9pm and Saturday 11am to 8pm. Brewery tours are held each Friday and Saturday and can be booked on their website. www.fourpure.com

Fourpure are one of the larger brewers situated in the Bermondsey area, with much of their equipment bought from the award winning Purity brewery in Warwickshire. They produce a number of beers that enjoy a good distribution in 330ml cans, being one of the first UK craft brewers to start selling in this format. At their taproom you'll find their three core beers; Pils Lager, Session IPA and American Pale, along with a selection from their Adventure Series beers, which include sours, porters, red ales and some very strong IPA's. There are usually around 14 beers available on draft and a selection of cans to choose from. On Saturday's food is often available from a local street food vendor. Brewery tours are held on Friday and Saturday and include a taste of 6 different beers from the Fourpure range. Details for booking these are on their website.

NEARBY: EeBria Taproom, 15 Almond Rd, SE16 3LR is a distributor of craft beer that opens its doors to the public on Saturday from 11am to 5.30pm, allowing people to try some of their stock. You'll normally find 6 beers from different independent craft brewers on draft and over 50 beers in bottles. www.eebria.com

Being located in Bermondsey, which has rather become a bit of a beer magnet, you'll find a number of other brewery taps within a 25 minute walk. The nearest to Fourpure are

Partizan Brewing at 8 Almond Rd, Bermondsey SE16 3LR and Brew By Numbers, 79 Enid St, Bermondsey SE16 3RA.

FULLERS, The Griffin Brewery, Chiswick Lane, Chiswick, W4 2QB. Approx 20minute walk from Turnham Green Tube. Brewery tours can be booked Monday to Saturday between 11am to 3pm, see website for details. The brewery shop is open to the public Monday to Friday 10am to 8pm and Saturday 10am to 3pm, selling a wide range of Fullers beers and merchandise. www.fullers.co.uk

Fullers is somewhat of a London institution. They actually have a beer named 1845 that celebrates the year that the Fullers Brewery was founded, although beer had been brewed on the site for many years prior to that. Their celebrated Griffin Brewery in Turner Green is both the largest and oldest in London and is well worth a visit. On the tour you get to see behind the scenes at the brewery, taste the beer and have the chance to have your photo taken behind the traditional pub-style bar in their tasting room. You'll also discover that their beers are much more varied than their ever-popular London Pride, with the nice Black Cab Stout, session ale Chiswick and American style Montanta Red all available to try.

NEARBY: If you are feeling hungry after the tour a Fullers pub, The Mawson Arms, is located next door to the brewery offering the full range of beers and good food. www.mawsonarmschiswick.co.uk

While in Chiswick it's worth checking out The Italian Job, which was the first Italian craft beer pub to open in the UK. Located about a 15 minute walk from the brewery at 13 Devonshire Road, Chiswick W4 2EU you'll find around 10 different Italian beers on draft along with a decent bottle selection. Food is also served. www.theitalianjobpub.co.uk

Fullers Brewery, Chiswick

GIPSY HILL BREWERY, Unit 11 Hamilton Road Industrial Estate, 160 Hamilton Road, Gipsy Hill SE27 9SF. Approximately 10 minutes walk to Gipsy Hill National Rail Train or 15 minutes walk to Sydenham Hill National Rail Train Station. Alternatively a 25 minute walk from Crystal Palace London Overground station. Taproom and Bottle Shop open every Saturday 12noon to 5pm. Brewery tours are not currently held. www.gipsyhillbrew.com
Situated on an industrial park in Gipsy Hill this craft brewer is proud of its South London roots, even offering a local

discount if you live within a mile of the brewery. The core beer range includes Southpaw Amber Ale, Beatnik Pale Ale, Dissident English Porter and Hepcat Session IPA. Additionally they produce a large number of experimental and seasonal brews. The brewery also own the Douglas Fir pub which is a 30 minute walk away (or jump on the train one stop from Gipsy Hill to Crystal Palace) at 144 Anerley Rd, Anerley, SE20 8DL. This bar initially opened in 2015 as a pop-up pub, but it is now open permanently. You'll find a good selection of their beers on draft along with a range of rotating guest beers.

NEARBY: Situated on the same industrial estate you'll also find The London Beer Factory, in fact you pass it in Unit 4 as you enter the estate. This brewery taproom is normally open on Saturday from 1pm to 6pm, so is well worth a visit if you are in the area. www.thelondonbeerfactory.com
Located about a 10 minute walk away is Beer Rebellion, 126 Gipsy Hill, SE19 1PL. This specialist craft beer bar is well worth seeking out, stocking an ever-changing draught list with 6 cask ales, 6 keg lines, and 2 ciders, as well as a large list of bottles. www.beerrebellion.org

GORGEOUS BREWERY, The Bull, 13 North Hill, Highgate, N6 4AB. Approximately 10 minutes walk from Highgate Tube. The brewery is located inside The Bull pub which is open Sunday to Thursday 12noon to 11pm, Friday 12noon to midnight and Saturday 10am to midnight. Brewery tours are not held, but the beers are available at the bar. www.gorgeousbrewery.com / www.thebullhighgate.co.uk
This smart pub in Highgate, that was previously the site of the London Brewing Company, is now home to the modestly named Gorgeous Brewery. This independent, family owned brewery produce a number of interesting beers, including Gravedigger Vanilla Milk Stout, Geek Hunter Extra Pale Ale and Greaseball APA. You'll normally find a selection of around 5 from their range on draft at the bar. The pub also offers a very good food menu, which is served all day.

NEARBY: Highgate is home to a number of interesting and historic pubs. For beer the Duke's Head at 16 Highgate High Street N6 5JG is probably best, which is around a 10 minute walk from The Bull. This former coaching inn stocks 8 ever changing Real Ales, 9 keg beers and a range of bottles and cans. The pub is owned by the same company that own The Prince in Wood Green which contains The House micro-brewery (see Bohem Brewery for details). As a result you can expect a few beers to normally come from their range. www.thedukesheadhighgate.co.uk

GOSNELLS MEAD BREWERY, Unit 2, Print Village, Chadwick Rd, Peckham SE15 4PU. Approximately 10 minutes walk from Peckham Rye London Overground Station. Taproom open every Saturday 12noon to 8pm. Brewery tours are normally held once a month, details can be found on their website. www.gosnells.co.uk

If you fancy a change from beer, this innovative brewery has been set up to try and popularise the ancient fermented honey drink of mead. Founded in 2013 the meadery produces a range of core drinks as well as seasonal experiments. Two of their recent drinks have included the addition of hops to the brewing process, resulting in some highly original and unusual tipples. The taproom is open at the brewery every Saturday giving you the opportunity to try their various creations and a tour of the brewery is normally held on a Saturday once a month. Full details are given on their website.

NEARBY: The Brick Brewery is located just around 5 minutes walk away, situated under the Peckham Rye station at Arch 209, Blenheim Grove, Peckham, SE15 4QL. You'll find around 9 of their beers on draft in their taproom along with a selection of cans and bottles. www.brickbrewery.co.uk

A 15 minute walk away you'll find John the Unicorn, 157-159 Rye Lane, SE15 4TL. This unusually named pub is owned by the Antic Group who in turn own the Croydon based Volden Brewery, so you'll find their range on draft along with a selection of guest and craft beers. Food is also served. www.johntheunicorn.com. Sadly Volden don't have a taproom or brewery tour, but their beers are definitely worth a try if you come across one of their predominately South London Antic pubs.

THE HAMMERTON BREWERY, Unit 8 & 9 Roman Way Industrial Estate, 149 Roman Way, Islington, N7 8XH. Approximately 2 minutes walk from Caledonian Road & Barnsbury London Overground Station. Alternatively a 15 minute walk from either Caledonian Road or Highbury & Islington Tube stations. Taproom open once a month, see website for details. Brewery tours are not currently held but brewing equipment is on display at the taproom. www.hammertonbrewery.co.uk

Hammerton Brewery was originally an old London brewery founded in 1868. Sadly it ceased to brew in the late 1950s after being taken over by Charrington in 1951. In 2014, a member of the Hammerton family decided to resurrect the family name in brewing and this small batch micro-brewery was started in an industrial unit near to Caledonian Road & Barnsbury station. The brewery produce 5 regular beers including N7 IPA, N1 Pale Ale and Pentonville Oyster Stout. In addition they brew a number of seasonal and experimental beers. You'll normally find around 9 different brews on draft when the taproom is open. If the dates for the monthly taproom opening don't suit you, the brewery have now opened their own pub less than 1km away from the brewery. The House of Hammerton at 97-99 Holloway Road, N7 8LT serves over 20 beers on draft including its own range and a selection of guests. In addition you'll also find over 50 bottles/cans available.

NEARBY: The Highbury Brewhouse and Kitchen is around a 15 minute walk, close to Highbury & Islington Tube, at 2a Corsica Street, N5 1JJ. This popular brewpub is part of a small chain that each has its own in-house brewer producing a range of beers to be served on draft. Good food is available. www.brewhouseandkitchen.com

The Cuckoo gastropub is around a 5 minute walk from the brewery at 115 Hemingford Road, London N1 1BZ. This interesting pub offers chefs a limited time pop-up restaurant opportunity, so you'll find the menu totally changes regularly when a different chef comes in. Beer wise The Cuckoo is owned by the Ripple Stream microbrewery, which is based on a Kent farm. You don't often see their beers on draft in London so it's nice to have their range on rotation behind the bar.

HAWKES CIDERY, 96 Druid St, Bermondsey, SE1 2HQ. Approximately 10 minutes walk to Bermondsey Tube or 20 minutes walk to London Bridge Tube and National Rail Train Station. Taproom open Wednesday to Friday 4pm to 11pm, Saturday 11am to 11pm and Sunday 11am to 6pm. www.wearehawkes.com
Okay we realise this isn't a brewery, but as it's located in the heart of the Bermondsey Beer Mile we thought we should include it as a bonus. Just to explain, the Bermondsey Beer Mile refers to the large amount of micro-breweries located close together in railway arches and industrial units in that area of London. Hawkes was London's first ever urban cidery. Their dedicated cider taproom offers a rotating menu of world craft ciders alongside their own Urban Orchard and Hawkes Ginger Beer range. A pizza based food menu is also served.

NEARBY: The Bermondsey Bottle Shop is located just a couple of minutes away at 128 Druid St, London SE1 2HH. Open Friday to Sunday this beer bar and shop normally has around 12 beers on tap and 400 in bottles. See their website for full details: www.bottleshop.co.uk
Additionally there are four other brewery taps within 5-10 minutes' walk; Anspach & Hobday, 118 Druid Street, SE1 2HH; Southwalk Brewing Company, 46 Druid St, SE1 2EZ; UBREW, Old Jamaica Business Estate, 29 Old Jamaica Rd, SE16 4AW; Brew By Numbers, 79 Enid St, SE16 3RA.

HIVER BEERS, 56 Stanworth St, Bermondsey SE1 3NY. Approximately 10 minutes walk to Bermondsey Tube or 20 minutes walk to London Bridge Tube and National Rail Train Station. Taproom open Friday 4pm to 10pm, Saturday 11am to 8pm and Sunday 11am to 6pm. Closed Monday to Thursday. Hive are a specialised honey beer brewer, so rather than a brewery tour, Hive offer a Hiver

Experience day on weekends and occasional Fridays. This day involves learning about urban bee keeping, inspecting a bee hive, followed by a tutored beer and food matching session. This is held at Bee Urban London, Kennington Park, St Agnes Place, SE11 4BE, full details are on their website. www.hiverbeers.com

Hiver are a craft brewery that specialises in honey beer, producing the blonde Hiver Honey Beer and the darker Hiver Honey Ale. You'll find these on draft at their taproom along with a selection of bottled beers. Hiver are located on the Bermondsey Beer Mile, which refers to an area of Bermondsey densely populated with breweries and taprooms. It's a great idea to combine you're visit to Hiver with another one (or several) of the other breweries in the vicinity.

NEARBY: The Bermondsey Bottle Shop is located just a few minutes away at 128 Druid St, London SE1 2HH. Open Friday to Sunday this beer bar and shop normally has around 12 beers on tap and 400 in bottles. See their website for full details: www.bottleshop.co.uk

Additionally there are four other brewery taps within 5-10 minutes' walk; Anspach & Hobday, 118 Druid Street, SE1 2HH; Southwalk Brewing Company, 46 Druid St, SE1 2EZ; UBREW, Old Jamaica Business Estate, 29 Old Jamaica Rd, SE16 4AW; Brew By Numbers, 79 Enid St, SE16 3RA.

HOPSTUFF BREWERY, Unit 7 Gunnery Terrace Woolwich, SE18 6SH. Approximately 10 minutes walk from Woolwich Arsenal DLR and National Rail Train Station. The brewery has a Taproom bar located a few minutes' walk away at 15 Major Draper St, SE18 6GD, which is open Monday to Thursday 4pm to 11pm, Friday & Saturday 12noon to midnight and Sunday 12noon to 10pm. www.hopstuffbrewery.com / www.taproomse18.com

The Hopstuff Brewery was formed after a successful crowd-funding campaign back in 2013. They produce a core range of beers including Four Hour Session IPA, Unfiltered Pils, APA and Renegade IPA, as well as a selection of seasonal and one-off beers. The actual brewery is open occasionally for special events so keep an eye on their website for details of these. Otherwise you can head to their Taproom bar located a street away from the brewery. This craft beer specialist bar was opened in 2015 and has all the Hopstuff beers on draft along with a large selection of guest beers in bottles and cans. Food is available, predominately sourdough pizza's and snacks.

NEARBY: The Dial Arch is practically next door at Number 1 Street, The Warren, Royal Arsenal Riverside, SE18 6GH. This impressive Young's Pub is located in the former Royal Arsenal complex dating from 1720. You'll find around 6 real ales on draft and a bottles. Good food is available. www.dialarch.com
A 5 minute walk leads you to another impressive pub housed in a historic building; The Woolwich Equitable is located at Equitable House, 10 Woolwich New Road, SE18 6AB. As the name suggests this Grade II listed building is the former headquarters of the Woolwich Equitable Building Society which was built in 1935. The pub is owned by the Antic chain who operate the Croydon based Volden Brewery. You'll find the Volden range of ales on draft along with a selection of guest and craft beers. Food is also served. Sadly Volden don't have a taproom or brewery tour, but their beers and interesting venues make their predominately South London Antic pubs always worth a visit. www.woolwichequitable.com

HOWLING HOPS BREWERY, Unit 9, Queens Yard, White Post Lane, E9 5EN. Approximately 5 minutes walk from Hackney Wick London Overground. Alternatively a 20 minute walk from one of Stratford Tube, DLR, London Overground and National Rail Train Station or Stratford International DLR and National Rail Train Station or Homerton London Overground station. Taproom open Sunday to Thursday 12noon to 11pm and Friday & Saturday 12noon to midnight. www.howlinghops.co.uk
This modern brewery started out in the basement of a nearby pub in 2011, but after outgrowing that site they moved to this industrial warehouse unit in 2015. Ten different beers are generally available, which are innovatively dispensed directly from large metal tanks

behind the bar. Regular brews include a Pale, IPA, Stout and Lager with other tanks offering seasonal and limited edition brews. Brewery tours are not currently offered, but all the brewing kit and materials are on display with helpful staff happy to answer any questions you may have. A limited food menu, predominantly burgers, is available.

NEARBY: The Crate Brewery is located practically next door on the same industrial park so it would be rude not to visit them while you are in the area. You'll can't miss them at Unit 7, Queens Yard, E9 5EN.
The Hackney based Five Points Brewery own the Mason and Company bar a 15 minute walk away on the opposite side of the canal at 25 East Bay Lane, Here East, Queen Elizabeth Olympic Park, E20 3BS. This impressive bar stocks around 20 types of craft beer on draft along with a large range of cans and bottles.

Howling Hops, Hackney Wick

LAINES BREWING, operated out of two brewpubs;
The Four Thieves, 51 Lavender Gardens, Clapham SW11
1DJ. Approximately 10 minutes walk from Clapham
Junction London Overground and National Rail Train
Station. Open Monday to Thursday 12noon to midnight,
Friday & Saturday 12noon to 2am and Sunday 12noon to
10.30pm. www.fourthieves.pub
The People's Park Tavern, 360 Victoria Park Rd, Hackney
E9 7BT. Approximately 15 minutes walk from Homerton
London Overground station. Open Sunday to Thursday
12noon to midnight, Friday 12noon to 2am and Saturday
11am to 2am. www.peoplesparktavern.pub
Laines are a London based pub company operating 17
very distinct and individual pubs around the capital. 2 of
these pubs have their own in-house brewery to produce
their own beers. Regular Laines brews include an IPA,
RPA (Random Pale Ale), ESB and a Porter, but what is
served does vary between pubs depending on what the in-
house brewery has been working on. This can include
seasonal and experimental brews. At the Four Thieves in
Clapham you'll find regular comedy, quizzes and band
nights are held, check their website for details. The
People's Park Tavern also holds regular events such as
quizzes and dj's, but is most noted for its fantastic beer
garden. Food is served at both pubs.
Laines also owns The Aeronaut brewpub in Acton. Sadly
this pub (which features comedy and circus shows) was
damaged in a fire at the start of 2017 and is being rebuilt,
but they hope to re-open soon. See their website for the
latest details. www.laines.london.

LONDON BEER FACTORY, 160 Hamilton Rd, West
Norwood, SE27 9SF. Approximately 10 minutes walk to
Gipsy Hill National Rail Train Station or 15 minutes walk to
Sydenham Hill National Rail Train Station. Alternatively a
25 minute walk from Crystal Palace London Overground
station. Taproom and Shop normally open every Saturday
1pm to 6pm. Brewery tours are not currently held.
www.thelondonbeerfactory.com
The London Beer Factory was founded in 2014 by brothers
Ed and Sim Cotton. They produce a core range of five

beers which include Chelsea Blond, Beyond the Pale and Paxton IPA. In addition they brew a Pilot Range of experimental beers each month. At the taproom you'll find the beers available on draft keg, but also in the innovative 360 can format, in which the complete top of the can is removed so it feels more like you are drinking from a glass rather than out of tin. The brewery has also converted a traditional black London cab into their Beer Cab, which is fitted with 8 taps on the side to dispense their beer. Occasionally ticket only events are held at the taproom at the weekend, such as sporting events on their big screen, so check their website to make sure they are open before you travel.

NEARBY: Situated on the same Industrial park at unit 11 you'll find the Gipsy Hill Brewery. Their taproom is normally open on Saturdays from 12noon to 5pm, so it's silly not to pay them a visit if you are in the vicinity. www.gipsyhillbrew.com
Located about a 10 minute walk away is Beer Rebellion, 126 Gipsy Hill, SE19 1PL. This specialist craft beer bar is definitely worth seeking out, stocking an ever-changing draught list with 6 cask ales, 6 keg lines, and 2 ciders, as well as a large list of bottles. www.beerrebellion.org

THE LONDON BREWING CO., 762 High Road, North Finchley, N12 9QH. Approximately 15 minute walk from Woodside Park Tube. Based inside The Bohemia Pub which is open Monday to Wednesday 12noon to 11pm, Thursday 12noon to Midnight, Friday and Saturday 12noon to 1am and Sunday 12noon to 10:30pm. Brewery tours are not currently held but the brewing equipment is all visible at the rear of the pub. www.thebohemia.co.uk / www.londonbrewing.com
The London Brewing Co. are a microbrewery based at the rather grand Bohemia Pub in North Finchley. Their 6.5 UK Barrel (10 hectolitre) brew kit sits on display at the lower rear of the pub and can produce up to 1800 pints per week. In the bar you'll normally find around 24 beers on draft, which will include up to 10 produced onsite along with a selection of guests. There is also a very good

selection of bottled and canned beers. The core range of London Brewing Co. drinks include a Pale Ale, IPA, Best Bitter, Wheat Beer and APA, but they also produce an interesting selection of one-off brews including sour and fruit beers. The Bohemia used to be an O'Neills Irish theme pub, but the faux interior was thrown out in 2014 to create this impressive stripped back, modern, open plan brewpub. The food menu is predominately US orientated with burgers and hotdogs, and they also do a good Sunday lunch.

NEARBY: About a mile further up the High Street you'll find The Griffin at 1262 High Road, Whetstone, N20 9HH. This famous old pub was built in 1928 although there has previously been an inn on the site for centuries, with the area being an important stopping point for coaches heading north from London. The current pub offers around 5 real ales on pump, a good food menu and there is a large, well kept beer garden for sunny days. www.griffinwhetstone.pub

THE LONG ARM BREW PUB, 20-26 Worship Street, Shoreditch, EC2A 2DX. Approximately 10 minutes walk from Old Street, Moorgate or Liverpool Street Tube and National Rail Train Stations. The pub is open Monday to Wednesday 11am to midnight, Thursday to Saturday 11am to 2am and Sunday from 11am to 11pm. Brewery tours are not currently held. www.longarmpub.com / www.longarmbrewing.co.uk

This centrally located gastro-pub only opened in 2017, although Long Arm has been brewing in a pub in Ealing for several years. This impressive brewpub set-up serves 6 beers directly from giant 1,000 litre tanks straight to the glass. The beers usually consist of the 4 core brews, Birdie Flipper Red Ale, IPA OK, Lucky Penny Pale Ale & Shadow Wolf Smoked Stout, along with 2 ever changing experiment brews. There's also a small selection of guest craft beers in bottles and cans. The brewery is overseen by Guillermo Alvarez Schulenburg, who is a third generation brewer from Mexico, where his Grandfather was the brewer and distributor of Corona and his uncle is the owner of three US breweries and distribution companies. The food menu is mainly burgers and hotdogs.

NEARBY: The Singer Tavern is so called as it's located inside the building that was once the former HQ of the Singer sewing machines at 1 City Rd, EC1Y 1AG. It's just a few minutes' walk from The Long Arm and it's well worth popping in as you'll find around 25 beers on draft, and if you add in the bottles/cans there are over 100 to choose from in total. Food is served, although it can get rather busy in the evenings so you may struggle to find a table. There is also a downstairs cocktail bar, that also keep a pretty good selection of beers. www.singertavern.com.

If you head north out of The Long Arm towards Old Street you'll find Old Fountain just over a 10 minute walk away at 3 Baldwin Street, EC1V 9NU. This old fashioned back street pub serves up an impressive 7 real ales on pump, along with a large selection of keg beers and bottles, mostly from local independent microbreweries. Food is available. www.facebook.com/OldFountain.

The other Long Arm brew pub is The Ealing Park Tavern, 222 South Ealing Road, W5 4RL. Approximately a 10 minute walk to South Ealing Tube station. Open Monday to Wednesday 11am to 11pm, Thursday to Saturday 11am to midnight and Sunday 12noon to 10.30pm. www.ealingparktavern.co.uk.

This traditional gastro-pub is housed in a restored old coaching inn. The onsite micro-brewery produce 4 core beers to be sold in the pub along with seasonal specials. Good food is served, including a highly recommended Sunday Roast.

MAGIC SPELLS BREWERY, 24 Rigg Approach, Leyton, E10 7QN. Approximately 10 minutes walk from Lea Bridge National Rail Train Station. Alternatively a 25 minute walk to Clapton London Overground station. Taproom and bottle shop open Tuesday to Sunday 10am to 4pm. Closed Monday. Opening hours maybe extended when special events are happening at the brewery, check out their website for details. Brewery tours are not currently held. www.magicspellsbrewery.co.uk

Magic Spells Brewery made the progression from home brewers to a 10 barrel kit on an industrial park in East London in 2016. They produce a number of core beers such as their Craft Lager, Hackney Hare Pale Ale and a hoppy IPA, as well as a number of experiment one-off and seasonal brews. At the taproom you'll find their beers on draft and bottled, as well as an impressive bottle and can shop stocking a very large range of other craft beers for take-away. Regular events are held at the brewery, such as DJ's, Classic Car Meets and street food. Check their website for details.

NEARBY: There are two other breweries nearby but at the time of writing neither have a formal taproom or tour. However they do both hold regular special events and beer launches so it's worth checking their websites to see if they are open. Nirvana Brewery, Unit T6, Leyton Industrial Village, Argall Avenue, E10 7QP is a 20 min walk from Magic Spells. Opened in 2017 Nirvana specialise in brewing tasty low and non-alcoholic beers. www.nirvanabrewery.com

Signature Brew are around a 25 minute walk at Unit 25, Leyton Business Centre, Etloe Road, E10 7BT. This brewery produces a number of music inspired beers with the aim of improving the choice behind the bar at gig venues. Beers include Roadie IPA, Backstage IPA, Stagediver (a 7.2% double IPA), along with some collaboration beers with bands such as The Slaves. www.signaturebrew.co.uk

MEANTIME, Brewery & Visitor Centre, Lawrence Trading Estate, Blackwall Lane, Greenwich, SE10 0AR. Approximately 20 minutes walk from North Greenwich Tube or 25 minutes walk from Cutty Sark DLR station. Alternatively 15 minutes walk from Westcombe Park or Maze Hill National Rail Train Stations. Taproom open Monday to Wednesday 12noon to 10.30pm, Thursday & Friday 12noon to 11pm, Saturday 11am to 11pm and Sunday 12noon to 6pm. Two hour brewery tours are

available to book online via their website. www.meantimebrewing.com
Since forming in 2000 the Meantime brewery has been a real success on the London brewing scene, with their beers now available all over the world. As part of that success story the brewery was been taken over firstly by SABMiller and then the Japanese Asahi Breweries. As with the Camden Town Brewery, some commentators have questioned whether being owned by a multinational conglomerate means that they forfeit their "Craft" credentials, whereas others argue that having larger owners simply opens up more opportunities to get their beer to a wider audience. We'll let you decide the answer to that debate. In the Tasting Room you'll find all the major Meantime beers such as London Lager, Pale Ale and Yakima Red, alongside a selection of seasonal and limited editions. The draft beers are all served straight from large metal maturation tanks to ensure they are fresh. Food is also served in the Tasting Room and there is a brewery shop attached so you can buy bottles to take away. Brewery tours are available every day and can be booked in advance through their website.

NEARBY: Greenwich has a number of lovely pubs. Two with riverside views, decent food and beer are The Cutty Sark, 4-6 Ballast Quay, Greenwich, SE10 9PD and The Trafalgar Tavern, 27 Park Row, SE10 9NW. www.cuttysarkse10.co.uk / www.trafalgartavern.co.uk
The Meantime brewery own The Greenwich Union pub at 56 Royal Hill, London SE10 8RT, which is around a 30 minute walk from the brewery. You'll find all the Meantime range on draft along with an interesting selection of up to 150 other beers from around the world. www.greenwichunion.com

MONCADA BREWERY, 37 Humber Rd, London NW2 6EN. The brewery is just over a 30 minute walk from Neasden, Dollis Hill or Willesden Green Tube stations or a 25 minute walk from Cricklewood National Rail Train Station. Busses also run nearby from Brent Cross and Kilburn Tube stations. Taproom open Friday 5pm to 11pm and Saturday 12noon to 9pm. Takeaway bottles can be purchased Monday to Thursday 10am to 4pm and Friday 10am to 10.30pm. Open hours may vary over the winter, check website for latest details. Brewery tours and not currently held. www.moncadabrewery.co.uk

Founded in 2011 by Julio Moncada, the brewery has come a long way in a few years and now produce a core range of 11 different beers, alongside a number of one-off and seasonal brews. They have also moved a long way, now located in larger premise than the original brewery which was 3 miles away in Knotting Hill. They enjoy a good distribution in pubs around London, with the core beer names generally make reference to the original breweries location combined with the particular beer style, for example Notting Hill Pale, Notting Hill Amber, Notting Hill Stout etc. There are a few exceptions such as So Sori Julio, the nice saison-style beer that the other brewers created while the owner was on holiday. The fancy new taproom now looks down into the brewery where you'll find most of the range available on draft.

NEARBY: Sadly being located in an industrial area there is a bit of a shortage of decent watering holes nearby. However if you are heading towards Willesden Green you'll find Beer + Burger at 88 Walm Lane, NW2 4QY. Part of a small chain, this craft beer specialist stocks around 20 rotating beers on draft and a large bottle selection. As the name suggests there's also a decent burger menu. www.beerandburgerstore.com

Just up the road from Beer+Burger is The Queensbury at 110a Walm Lane, NW2 4RS. The food in this pub/restaurant is slightly more gourmet and you'll find a smaller but often interesting range of beer available. www.thequeensbury.co.uk

MONDO BREWERY, 86 Stewart's Road, Battersea, SW8 4UG. Approximately 20 minutes walk from Stockwell Tube. Alternatively 10 minutes from Wandsworth Road London Overground or 10 minutes from Battersea Park National Rail Train Station. Taproom open Wednesday to Friday 5pm to 11pm and Saturday 2pm to 10pm. Tours are regularly held on Saturdays, email for details. www.mondobrewingcompany.com

This modern brewery started out in 2015 and produces an excellent range of regular and experimental beers. Full marks has to go to the imaginative beer names that include Dennis Hopp'r IPA, James' Brown Ale and Van Dammage Belgium IPA. The Taproom is located upstairs in a rather plain building on an industrial estate, but the trip is well worth it is as you'll find around 15 different beers on draft as well as a selection of bottles in the fridge.

Mondo Brewery, Wandsworth Road

NEARBY: Around a 10 minute walk will take you to The Priory Arms at 83 Lansdowne Way, SW8 2PB. This fantastic pub always stocks around 70 beers on draft and in bottles, including a good Belgium range, so you really are spoilt for choice. Food is also available. www.theprioryarms.com

The Bread & Roses pub is a 20 minute walk from the brewery at 68 Clapham Manor Street, Clapham, SW4 6DZ. This interesting venue is owned by The Battersea and Wandsworth Trade Union Council and as well as a pub features a theatre, comedy club and live music. You'll normally find a good range of beer and food is available. www.breadandrosespub.com

ORBIT BEERS, Arch 228, Fielding St, Kennington, SE17 3HD. Approximately 15 minutes walk from Kennington Tube or 15 minutes to Elephant & Castle National Rail Train Station. Alternatively a 20 minute walk from Elephant & Castle Tube. The Taproom is open every Saturday from 12noon to 8pm. Brewery tours are not currently held. www.orbitbeers.com
Started in 2014 you'll find the Orbit microbrewery located in the ever popular railway arch. The brewery produce a number of different beers, but tend to focus on European styles such as their Peel Belgian Pale, Neu Dusseldorf style Altbier and Nico a Cologne style Kolsch. At the brewery taproom/shop you'll find the core beers on draft along with any one-off brews they have been working on. The beers are also available in bottles if you want to take them away. Special events are held at the brewery throughout the year, check their website or Facebook page for latest details.

NEARBY: Mamuśka is a 15 minute walk at 16 Elephant and Castle, SE1 6TH. This Polish kitchen and bar serves up hearty portions of traditional Polish cuisine, such as delicious Pork Gulasz (goulash) or Pan Fried Trout. You'll also find around 15 different Polish beers available in bottles, alongside an impressive selection of vodkas. www.mamuska.net
Oaka at The Mansion House is a 15 minute walk from the brewery at 48 Kennington Park Rd, SE11 4RS. This bar/restaurant is owned by the Peterborough based brewery Oakham Ales. The concept is Pan-Asian dining accompanied by a decent pint of beer. And a jolly good concept it is too. If you aren't feeling hungry there is a bar

area, so you can just try their beers out. www.oakalondon.com

The White Bear pub is along the road from Oaka at 138 Kennington Park Rd, SE11 4DJ. This friendly pub normally has a good selection of beers available on draft as well as range of London-based craft beers in bottles. Good food is served and there is also a small theatre upstairs that puts on some interesting shows. www.whitebearkennington.co.uk

PARTIZAN BREWING, 8 Almond Rd, Bermondsey SE16 3LR. Approximately 10 minutes walk to Bermondsey Tube or 15 minutes walk to Surrey Quays London Overground station. Taproom open Saturday 11am to 8pm (may close earlier during the winter, check website for details). Brewery tours are not currently offered. www.partizanbrewing.co.uk

This craft microbrewery was founded in 2012 and brew a number of interesting beers, that are notable for their funky labels. The brewery use label artist Alec Doherty who creates distinctive designs using a fusion of Soviet, modern European and 1960's US counterculture influences. Current beers include a Lemongrass Saison and Lemon & Thyme Saison, both of which are well worth trying. The Taproom normally has 4 different beers on draft and a selection of bottles available.

NEARBY: Located on the same street you'll find the EeBria Taproom, 15 Almond Rd, SE16 3LR. This trade distributor of craft beer opens its doors on Saturdays from 11am to 5.30pm to allow the public to buy some of their stock. You'll normally find 6 beers from different independent craft brewers on draft and over 50 different beers in bottles. www.eebria.com

Being located in Bermondsey, which has rather become a bit of a beer magnet, you'll find a number of other brewery taps all within a 15-20 minute walk. These include; Fourpure, 22 Bermondsey Trading Estate, Rotherhithe New Rd, SE16 3LL; UBREW, Old Jamaica Business Estate, 29 Old Jamaica Rd, SE16 4AW; Brew By Numbers, 79 Enid St, SE16 3RA. The Kernel Brewery,

Arch 11 Dockley Road Industrial Estate, SE16 3SF is also about a 10 minute walk. Sadly they do not have a taproom or tour, but they are open 9am to 2pm on Saturday selling bottles to take-away. www.thekernelbrewery.com

REDCHURCH BREWERY, 275-276 Poyser St, Bethnal Green, E2 9RF. Approximately 5 minutes walk from Cambridge Heath London Overground station. Alternatively a 10 minute walk from Bethnal Green Tube. The brewery Taproom is open Thursday and Friday 6pm to 12.30am and Saturday 12noon to 12.30am. Brewery tours are not currently held. www.redchurch.beer
You'll find Redchurch located in a railway arch in a back street behind Cambridge Heath station. This busy microbrewery has recently expanded and now has a second brewing site in Essex. The brewery uses two brands, the main Redchurch, producing the core range such as Brick Lane Lager, Shoreditch Blonde and the rather nice (but rather alcoholic) Great Eastern IPA. The other brand, Urban Farmhouse, is used for more experimental and one-off brews, such as their interesting cherry and plum sour beers. They don't currently offer a brewery tour but there are regular events and talks at their taproom, check their Twitter or Facebook page for details. In the taproom you'll find around 10 different beers on draft along with a range of bottles. DJ's and streetfood vendors are a frequent addition in the evenings.

NEARBY: Mother Kelly's is a 10 minute walk away at 251 Paradise Row, Bethnal Green, E2 9LE. This impressive specialist beer bar is part of a small chain and serves 20 beers on tap alongside 6 large fridges full of weird and wonderful bottles from across the globe. www.motherkellys.co.uk
In the other direction you'll find The Dove at 24-28 Broadway Market, E8 4QJ. This popular pub always has a good range of beer on draft along with a bottle selection of around 100. The emphasis is mainly on Belgium beers. Food is available. www.dovepubs.com

SAMBROOK'S BREWERY, Unit 1 & 2 Yelverton Road, Battersea, SW11 3QG. Approximately 15 minutes walk from Clapham Junction London Overground and National Rail Train Station. Taproom open 6pm to 10pm Thursday & Friday and 1pm to 10pm on Saturday. Brewery tours are held once a month on a Thursday and a Saturday, see website for details. www.sambrooksbrewery.co.uk

Formed in 2008 this rapidly growing brewery produces beers such as Junction, Battersea Rye and the lovely session beer Wandle. You'll find these in the taproom along and other seasonal brews such as Lavender Hill, which is brewed with lavender honey, and the complex 10.4% Russian Imperial Stout. Each summer the brewery organise the Beer on the Common festival in south London offering food, beer and music which is well worth attending. You'll find details about this and their regular brewery tours on their website.

NEARBY: It's about a 20 minute walk to The Draft House, 74-76 Battersea Bridge Rd, SW11 3AG. This small chain of pubs each offers an amazing range of drinks from around the world, so no beer connoisseur will be disappointed. Food is also available. www.drafthouse.co.uk

If you're heading towards Clapham Junction you'll find the impressive off-licence/bar We Brought Beer at 78 St John's Hill, SW11 1SF around a 20 minute walk away. This specialist beer shop is part of a small chain and stocks around 400 different beers in bottles and cans alongside 4 ever-changing beers on draft. All can be drunk in store or taken away. www.webroughtbeer.co.uk

SOUTHEY BREWING COMPANY, 21 Southey St, Penge SE20 7JD. Approximately 10 minutes walk from Penge West London Overground station. Alternatively a 10 minute walk from Penge East National Rail Train Station. Taproom open every Friday and Saturday 5pm to 10pm. Brewery tours are not currently held. www.southeybrewing.co.uk

Located in an old Victorian era warehouse, this relatively new microbrewery was opened in 2016 by the team of Sam Barber, Darren McCrae and Graham Lawrence.

Despite being new, they have good pedigree as Sam had previously been head brewer at the popular local brewery Late Knights that had sadly closed. They produce 6 core beers, an IPA, Best Bitter, Oatmeal Stout, Mild, Pale Ale and Session IPA, along with a range of experimental and one-off brews. They don't currently run brewery tours but the taproom is open every Friday and Saturday and you'll usually find the 5 or 6 of their beers on draft along with a guest real cider. A selection of bottled beers are also available. In addition to the taproom the brewery own a couple of pubs, one of which is located in London. The London Beer Dispensary at 389 Brockley Rd, Brockley SE4 2PH is imaginatively designed as a bar without a bar (yes, there really is no traditional bar counter), which serves up an impressive selection of beers straight from the barrel/keg. There is also a good range of bottles and canned beers available along with tasty burgers. www.facebook.com/LDNDispensary. The other pus is based in Brighton and located at Brighton Beer Dispensary, 38 Dean St, Brighton BN1 3EG. www.facebook.com/BRTNDispensary

NEARBY: A 10 minute walk leads to The Alexandra, 163 Parish Lane, Penge, SE20 7JH. This old pub re-opened in 2017 and now serves a range of interesting beers on draft, normally 3 real ales and 9 on keg, along with a good selection of bottles. Food is also served. www.facebook.com/TheAlexandraPenge
The Douglas Fir is a 20 minute walk away at 144 Anerley Rd, Anerley, SE20 8DL. This new bar initially opened in 2015 by the local Gipsy Hill Brewing Company as a pop-up pub, but it is now open permanently. You'll find a good selection of Gipsy Hill beers on draft along with a range of rotating guest beers. www.gipsyhillbrew.com

SOUTHWALK BREWING COMPANY, 46 Druid St, Bermondsey, SE1 2EZ. Approximately 15 minutes walk to Bermondsey Tube or 15 minutes walk to London Bridge Tube and National Rail Train Station. Taproom open Tuesday and Thursday 7pm to 10pm, Friday 5pm to 10pm, Saturday 11am to 6pm and Sunday 11am to 4pm. Closed

Monday and Wednesday. Brewery tours are held Thursday evenings and Saturday, see their website for details. www.southwarkbrewing.co.uk

If you are coming from London Bridge station this gem of a brewery will mark the start of the Bermondsey Beer Mile; a boozy brewery crawl that refers to the large amount of taprooms located close together in the railway arches and industrial units of this part of London. Southwalk Brewing Company predominately focus on cask beer rather than keg and you'll normally find at least 6 different types to try. Cask refers to the type of beer that is generally hand pulled from the barrel, rather than served with carbon dioxide added. It's the old traditional way to serve beer, with the liquid still maturing naturally in the cask from which it is served. The downside is that oxygen gets into the barrel as it is poured eventually making the beer flat and stale, meaning the cask has a shorter shelf-life than the keg alternative. People can debate for hours on the pros and cons of both styles so I'm going to say no more, but if you do a brewery tour be sure to ask the guide for their take on it.

NEARBY: The impressive Bermondsey Bottle Shop is located a few minutes' walk away at 128 Druid St, London SE1 2HH. Open Friday to Sunday this beer bar and shop normally has around 12 beers on tap and 400 in bottles. See their website for full details: www.bottleshop.co.uk

Additionally there are four other brewery taps within 5-10 minute walk; Hiver Beers, 56 Stanworth St, Bermondsey SE1 3NY; Anspach & Hobday, 118 Druid Street, SE1 2HH; Brew By Numbers, 79 Enid St, SE16 3RA; UBREW, Old Jamaica Business Estate, 29 Old Jamaica Rd, SE16 4AW.

TAP EAST, 7 International Square, Montfichet Road, Westfield Stratford City, E20 1EE. Approximately 10 minutes walk from Stratford Tube, DLR, London Overground and National Rail Train Stations. Alternatively a 5 minute walk from Stratford International DLR and National Rail Train Stations. Brewery taproom open Monday to Saturday 11am to 11pm and Sunday 12noon to 10pm. Brewery tours are not held, but you can see the

brewing equipment in a room at the back of the bar.
www.tapeast.co.uk

If only every shopping centre could have its very own specialist beer bar and microbrewery, just imagine how much more enjoyable shopping would become. Fortunately the planners who developed the massive Westfield Stratford City shopping mall were considerate enough to allow Tap East to set up shop. This impressive bar offers 16 ever changing beers on draft including Tap East brews and guests, as well as over 100 bottled beers from around the world. Core beers include IPA, East End Mild, APA and Coffee in the Morning; a dark stout brewed with ground coffee beans from the nearby Grind Coffee Bar. A fairly basic food menu is available.

NEARBY: Bat & Ball, Unit 1110/1111, Westfield Centre Stratford City, E20 1EJ is located in the same shopping centre. This interesting bar and restaurant concept contains 12 Ping Pong tables so you can have a game of table tennis while you drink. The beer menu contains over 50 craft beers, mainly in bottles. www.thebatandball.com

Also in the shopping centre you'll find Cow at 4 Chestnut Plaza, Westfield Stratford City, E20 1GL. This large gastro-pub normally has 8 real ales on draft alongside a selection of craft beers. www.thecowwestfield.co.uk

TWICKENHAM FINE ALES, 18 Mereway Road, Twickenham TW2 6RG. Approximately 20 minute walk from Twickenham or Strawberry Hill National Rail Train Stations. Brewery tours are held on the second Wednesday of each month and can be booked through their website. The brewery bar is open regularly before rugby matches (Twickenham is the home of the England and Harlequins rugby union teams). There is also a comedy night in the brewery once a month. A list of open days is available on the brewery website. www.twickenham-fine-ales.co.uk

Founded in 2004, when there were less than 10 breweries in London, Twickenham Fine Ales was a frontrunner for the current surge in independent microbreweries. Their range of award winning ales was a very welcome addition to the beer scene at the time and are still well worth seeking out today. The range now consists of 20 beers throughout the year; 4 regulars, 4 seasonal and 12 monthly specials. The core beers being Redhead, Naked Ladies, Sundancer and Grandstand. If you can't make a tour or one of the taproom openings the brewery has a shop where you can buy bottles and merchandise to take-away. This is open Monday to Friday 9am to 6pm and Saturday 10am to 1pm.

NEARBY: The Twickenham area has a number of very good and historic pubs. We've picked a couple of interesting ones but there are plenty more. The Sussex Arms is approximately a 5 minute walk from the brewery at 15 Staines Rd, TW2 5BG. This fantastic, beer focussed pub has 15 cask ale pumps, as well as 6 cider taps and 10 keg lines, along with over 100 bottled beers. Good food is also available. www.thesussexarmstwickenham.co.uk
A 20 minute will lead you to gastro pub Brouge at 241 Hampton Road, TW2 5NJ. This bar and bistro specialises in Belgian and Craft beers. There are 18 beers on tap along with around 50, predominately Belgian, bottles. Good food is available. www.brouge.co.uk

UBREW, Old Jamaica Business Estate, 29 Old Jamaica Rd, Bermondsey SE16 4AW. Approximately 10 minutes walk to Bermondsey Tube or 20 minutes walk to London Bridge Tube and National Rail Train Station. Taproom open Thursday to Saturday 12noon to 11pm and Sunday 12noon to 7pm. Closed Monday to Wednesday. As the name suggests, rather than a brewery tour, UBREW offers you the chance to brew. They hold one day training courses a couple of times a month with an experienced brewer talking you though the whole brewing process. You even get to drink the finished product once it has fermented. If you enjoy the experience you can pay a regular membership fee and come back every month and try brewing different types of beer. See their website for details. www.ubrew.cc
Not to worry if you don't fancy spending the day brewing at UBREW, they do brew their own range of beers which are available on draft in the taproom, which is open to the

public Thursday to Sunday. The beers served do vary, but normally include an IPA, Stout and Wheat beer. A word of caution though, UBREW are cash free so make sure you bring a bank card. Like several other entries in this book the brewery is located on the Bermondsey Beer Mile, a term that refers to the large amount of taprooms located close together in this part of London.

NEARBY: The Bermondsey Bottle Shop is located a few minutes' walk away at 128 Druid St, London SE1 2HH. Open Friday to Sunday this beer bar and shop normally has 12 beers on tap and 400 in bottles. See their website for full details: www.bottleshop.co.uk
Additionally there are four other brewery taps within 10 minutes walk; Brew By Numbers, 79 Enid St, SE16 3RA; Anspach & Hobday, 118 Druid Street, SE1 2HH; Hiver Beers, 56 Stanworth St, SE1 3NY; Southwalk Brewing Company, 46 Druid St, SE1 2EZ.

VILLAGES BREWERY, 21-22 Resolution Way, Deptford, SE8 4NT. Approximately 4 minutes walk to Deptford National Rail Train Station. Alternatively a 10 minute walk to Greenwich or Deptford Bridge DLR stations. Taproom open Friday 5pm to 11pm, Saturdays 12noon to 11pm. Brewery tours are not currently held. www.villagesbrewery.com
Villages are a small microbrewery located in two railway arches in Deptford. The brewery is owned by brothers Archie and Louis Village, which explains the brewery name, who started brewing at the end of 2016, initially with second hand equipment brought from Gipsy Hill Brewery. They open the taproom on Friday and Saturday and you'll normally find five beers available on draft as well as a range of cans and bottles. The core range includes Whistle Pilsner, Rodeo Pale Ale and Toucan Session IPA.
NEARBY: Around a 10 minute walk away you'll find The Dog and Bell, 116 Prince St, SE8 3JD. This is a fine old fashioned back street pub that has built up an enviable reputation for its beer. They have six handpumps selling real ale and a good range of bottled beers in the fridge. Food is available and they hold an annual Pickle Festival

each November, which is well worth attending if you like chutney and onions! www.facebook.com/TheDogandBell
Slightly closer (just around the corner from the brewery in fact) is the Job Centre, 120 Deptford High St, SE8 4NP. This modern pub is located, yes you guessed it, inside the old Job Centre building. It serves a good selection of beer, normally with 5 real ales on draft and a selection of bottles. Food is also served. www.jobcentredeptford.com

WILD CARD BREWERY, Unit 7, Ravenswood Industrial Estate, Shernhall Street, Walthamstow E17 7LG. Approximately 15 minutes walk from Walthamstow Central Tube or London Overground station. Alternatively 15 minutes walk from Wood Street London Overground station. Taproom open Friday 5pm to midnight, Saturday 11am to midnight and Sunday 11am to 11pm. Tours are regularly held on Saturdays, see website for details. www.wildcardbrewery.co.uk
Opened in 2014 this microbrewery produces five core beers; Joker Czech style Pilsner, Jack of Clubs ruby ale, Queen of Diamonds IPA, King of Hearts blonde beer and Ace of Spades London Porter, each with a distinctive playing card logo. If you visit the taproom you'll find these on draft along with local guest beers and a selection of bottles. Brewery tours are available as well as a brewery experience day, which can be booked via their website. Street Food vendors normally serve outside, details of these can also be found on their website. In 2017 the brewery expanded to a second brewing location around 2 miles away from the initial site. This is at Wild Card Brewery, Unit 2, Lockwood Way, Walthamstow, E17 5RB, which also features a taproom open Friday 5pm to midnight and Saturday 12noon to midnight. For visiting this site by public transport Blackhorse Road Tube and London Overground station is a 15 minute walk away.
NEARBY: Nag's Head, 9 Orford Road, Walthamstow, E17 9LP is only about a 5 minute walk away from the brewery. This friendly backstreet pub has 7 real ales on draft and food is served all day.
The unusually named Mirth, Marvel & Maud is a 15-20 minute walk from the brewery at 186 Hoe St,

Walthamstow, E17 4QH. This former cinema now houses a multi-purpose arts centre that also includes a restaurant and bar area. You'll normally find a good range of beers available, which are often from smaller London breweries. www.mirthmarvelandmaud.com

ZERODEGREES MICROBREWERY, 29-31 Montpelier Vale, Blackheath, SE3 0TJ. Approximately 5 minutes walk from Blackheath National Rail Train Station. Alternatively a 25 minute walk from Lewisham DLR station. The brewery is located within the Zerodegrees Restaurant Bar which is open Monday to Saturday 12noon to midnight and Sunday 12noon to 11pm. Brewery tours are not currently held. www.zerodegreesmicrobrewery.co.uk

Opened in 2000 this was the first of what is now a small chain of brewpub restaurants. The seating practically overlooks the brewing equipment and if you visit during the day you'll often see the team working on a brew. The core range consists of a Pilsner, Pale Ale, Wheat beer, Black lager and a refreshing Mango beer. They also brew a variety of special one-off beers throughout the year. The food is a good selection of wood fire pizzas, mussels and pasta. The other Zerodegrees branches are located in Bristol, Cardiff and Reading.

NEARBY: Located about 5 minutes away on the same road you'll find the Princess of Wales, 1a Montpelier Row, SE3 0RL. This popular pub always offers a good range of beers along with a decent food menu.

A 5-10 minute walk in the other direction will take you to the Hare & Billet, 1a Eliot Cottages, Hare & Billet Road, SE3 0QJ. This very beer focussed pub offers 10 hand pumps carrying beer from mostly local small breweries, along with real ciders & perries. This is in addition to the 12 rotating keg taps. Food is also available.

PUBLIC TRANSPORT INDEX

Tube, Rail, London Overground and DLR stations with Breweries and Taprooms nearby.

ACTON CENTRAL LONDON OVERGROUND
Dragonfly Brewery

ACTON TOWN TUBE
Dragonfly Brewery

ALDGATE TUBE
Alphabeta Brewery

ANGEL TUBE
Brewhouse and Kitchen Islington

BALHAM TUBE
Belleville Brewing Company

BATTERSEA PARK NATIONAL RAIL
Mondo Brewery

BERMONDSEY TUBE
Anspach & Hobday
Brew by Numbers
Fourpure Brewing
Hawkes Cidery
Hiver Beers
Partizan Brewing
Southwalk Brewing Company
UBREW

BETHNAL GREEN TUBE
Redchurch Brewery

BLACKFRIARS TUBE / NATIONAL RAIL
Essex Street Brewery

BLACKHEATH NATIONAL RAIL
Zerodegrees Microbrewery

BLACKHORSE ROAD TUBE / LONDON OVERGROUND
Wild Card Brewery (new site)

BOUNDS GREEN TUBE
Bohem Brewery
House Brewery (see Bohem Brewery)

BOWES PARK NATIONAL RAIL
Bohem Brewery
House Brewery (see Bohem Brewery)

BRIXTON TUBE / NATIONAL RAIL
Brixton Brewery
Bullfinch Brewery
Canopy Beer Company
Clarkshaws Brewery

BROCKLEY LONDON OVERGROUND / NATIONAL RAIL
Brockley Brewery Company

CALEDONIAN ROAD TUBE
The Hammerton Brewery

CALEDONIAN ROAD & BARNSBURY LONDON OVERGROUND
The Hammerton Brewery

CAMBRIDGE HEATH LONDON OVERGROUND
Redchurch Brewery

CAMDEN TOWN TUBE
Camden Town Brewery

CHALK FARM TUBE
Camden Town Brewery

CLAPHAM JUNCTION LONDON OVERGROUND / NATIONAL RAIL
Laines Brewing - The Four Thieves Pub
Sambrook's Brewery

CLAPTON LONDON OVERGROUND
Magic Spells Brewery

CRICKLEWOOD NATIONAL RAIL
Moncada

CRYSTAL PALACE LONDON OVERGROUND
Gipsy Hill Brewery
London Beer Factory

CUTTY SARK DLR
Meantime

DALSTON JUNCTION LONDON OVERGROUND
40ft Brewery

DALSTON KINGSLAND LONDON OVERGROUND
40ft Brewery

DEPTFORD NATIONAL RAIL
Villages Brewery

DEPTFORD BRIDGE DLR
Villages Brewery

DOLLIS HILL TUBE
Moncada

ELEPHANT & CASTLE TUBE / NATIONAL RAIL
Orbit Beers

ERITH NATIONAL RAIL
Bexley Brewery

GIPSY HILL NATIONAL RAIL
Gipsy Hill Brewery
London Beer Factory

GREENWICH DLR
Villages Brewery

HACKNEY CENTRAL LONDON OVERGROUND
Five Points Brewery

HACKNEY DOWNS NATIONAL RAIL
Five Points Brewery

HACKNEY WICK LONDON OVERGROUND
Crate
Howling Hops

HAYDONS ROAD NATIONAL RAIL
By The Horns Brewing Company

HERNE HILL NATIONAL RAIL
Bullfinch Brewery
Canopy Beer Company

HIGH BARNET TUBE
The Barnet Brewery

HIGHBURY & ISLINGTON TUBE / LONDON OVERGROUND /
NATIONAL RAIL
Brewhouse and Kitchen Highbury
The Hammerton Brewery

HIGHGATE TUBE
Gorgeous Brewery

HOMERTON LONDON OVERGROUND
Crate Brewery
Howling Hops Brewery
Laines Brewing - The People's Park Tavern Pub

KENNINGTON TUBE
Orbit Beers

KENTISH TOWN WEST LONDON OVERGROUND
Camden Town Brewery

LEA BRIDGE NATIONAL RAIL
Magic Spells Brewery

LEWISHAM DLR
Zerodegrees Microbrewery

LIVERPOOL STREET TUBE / NATIONAL RAIL
The Long Arm Brew Pub
Alphabeta Brewery

LONDON BRIDGE TUBE / NATIONAL RAIL
Anspach & Hobday
Brew by Numbers
Hawkes Cidery
Hiver Beers
Southwalk Brewing Company
UBREW

LOUGHBOROUGH JUNCTION NATIONAL RAIL
Brixton Brewery
Clarkshaws Brewery

MAZE HILL NATIONAL RAIL
Meantime

MOORGATE TUBE / NATIONAL RAIL
The Long Arm Brew Pub

NEASDEN TUBE
Moncada

NORTH DULWICH NATIONAL RAIL
Bullfinch Brewery
Canopy Beer Company

NORTH GREENWICH TUBE
Meantime

OLD STREET TUBE / NATIONAL RAIL
The Long Arm Brew Pub

PECKHAM RYE LONDON OVERGROUND / NATIONAL RAIL
Brick Brewery
Gosnells Mead Brewery

PENGE EAST NATIONAL RAIL
Southey Brewing Company

PENGE WEST LONDON OVERGROUND
Southey Brewing Company

PONDERS END NATIONAL RAIL
Camden Town Brewery (new site)

SLADE GREEN NATIONAL RAIL
Bexley Brewery

SOUTH BERMONDSEY NATIONAL RAIL
Fourpure Brewing

SOUTH EALING TUBE
The Long Arm Brewery - The Ealing Park Tavern

SOUTHBURY LONDON OVERGROUND
Camden Town Brewery (new site)

STOCKWELL TUBE
Mondo Brewery

STRATFORD TUBE / DLR / LONDON OVERGROUND /
NATIONAL RAIL
Crate Brewery
Howling Hops Brewery
Tap East

STRATFORD INTERNATIONAL DLR / NATIONAL RAIL
Crate Brewery
Howling Hops Brewery
Tap East

STRAWBERRY HILL NATIONAL RAIL
Twickenham Fine Ales

SURBITON NATIONAL RAIL
Big Smoke Brew Co.

SURREY QUAYS LONDON OVERGROUND
Fourpure Brewing
Partizan Brewing

SYDENHAM HILL NATIONAL RAIL
Gipsy Hill Brewery
London Beer Factory

TEMPLE TUBE
Essex Street Brewery

TOOTING BROADWAY TUBE
By The Horns Brewing Company

TOTTENHAM HALE TUBE / LONDON OVERGROUND
Bevertown Brewery

TULSE HILL NATIONAL RAIL
Bullfinch Brewery

TURNHAM GREEN TUBE
Fullers

TWICKENHAM NATIONAL RAIL
Twickenham Fine Ales

WALTHAMSTOW CENTRAL TUBE / LONDON OVERGROUND
Wild Card Brewery

WANDSWORTH COMMON NATIONAL RAIL
Bellevill Brewing Company

WANDSWORTH ROAD LONDON OVERGROUND
Mondo Brewery

WEST DULWICH NATIONAL RAIL
Bullfinch Brewery

WILLESDEN GREEN TUBE
Moncada

WESTCOMBE PARK NATIONAL RAIL
Meantime

WIMBLEDON PARK TUBE
By The Horns Brewing Company

WOOD GREEN TUBE
Bohem Brewery
House Brewery (see Bohem Brewery)

WOOD STREET LONDON OVERGROUND
Wild Card Brewery

WOODSIDE PARK TUBE
The London Brewing Co.

WOOLWICH ARSENAL DLR / NATIONAL RAIL

Bexley Brewery (plus bus journey)
Hopstuff Brewery

11028155R00039

Printed in Great Britain
by Amazon